Following
Civil War
Photographers

Acknowledgments

This book would not have been possible were it not for the brave combat photographers of the Civil War, some of which are portrayed in this book.

My gratitude to Allen Moore, a friend and mentor. My highest regard to William A. Frassanito who showed the way by identifying so many of the locations used by Civil War Photographers. I am indebted to the wonderful staff at the Prints and Photographic Division of the Library of Congress, National Archives, and the USMHI for helping me acquire so many of the prints seen in this book. My thanks to Kim Holien, Fort Historian for Fort McNair and Fort Myer, Washington D.C. and Virginia who provided so much useful information to identifying photographic sites around Washington D.C.. In addition, my appreciation to so many friendly, knowledgeable people such as Maria Washburn at the Historical Society of Frederick County, the staff at the Civil War Medicine Museum, Frederick, Maryland, Susan Cumby at the Fort Ward Museum, Arlington, Virginia, and Martha Bennett at Fort Delaware Society who helped me find individual prints so important to this book.

Most of all to my wife, Harvest, my undying appreciation for her support, patience, and keeping the home fires burning while I pursued my dream.

Foster

This first edition published in 2003 by

Jennings Sayre Publications
2341 Little Bighorn Dr.
Henderson, NV 89052

Library of Congress Control Number: 2003103296

Book and jacket designed by Ed Miranda

Printed and bound by C&C Offset Printing Co. Ltd, China

ISBN: 0-9729984-0-3

Following Civil War Photographers

Foster Eubank

Jennings Sayre Publications

Foreword

Growing up as a child during the Second World War, I was naturally aware of the subject of war and sensed the effect on American townsfolk. I remember the flag, with the star, in the window of those who had a loved one away fighting that war and the sacrifices being made. Simultaneously, I became aware of another war that occurred in America. A war of almost 80 years ago (at that time of my life) that was fought between Americans on American soil. I was puzzled, for in my boyish mind I was comparing World War II which was being fought overseas against obvious enemies to that of the Civil War which was fought between the states that made up the Union, between Northerners and Southerners, between neighbors, and even between family members. These not so obvious enemies lost over 600,000 lives.

As I grew into adulthood, I yearned to know more about the Civil War. I took to the books on the subject, reading everything I could get my hands on. Being a visually oriented person it was the photographic images taken during the war that captured my interest the most. The more I looked at those images the more I began to wonder where they were taken. I then begin to wonder if the same photographed locations still existed today and how they might appear. Being a Westerner, I was not within easy driving distance to the battlefields of the Civil War much less to the sites where the Civil War images were made, so I just had to let my imagination take me there and I continued to look at the photos and wonder. Then, as an adult, I got the good fortune to obtain a job which allowed me to travel to all the states where the Civil War was fought. With some free time, and camera in hand, I visited the battlefields and starting taking pictures. Now I was able to see those sites where the images that stirred my boyish imagination were taken and pretend I was a Civil War photographer like Matthew B. Brady, Alexander Gardner, Timothy H. O'Sullivan, Sam Cooley, or George Barnard.

About the time I was visiting the battlefields, Civil War historian, William A. Frassanito, made his creative, original, breakthrough books, which accurately identified the original sites of numerous Civil War photographs and correctly identified all pertinent information. Most importantly, Frassanito included the "then" photograph taken by the Civil War photographer and the "now" photograph which showed the same area as it looks today. With his books in hand, I was now able to find those photographed locations that had so stimulated my imagination, and not only seeing them, but photographing them. It is truly exciting to look for a photographic site and then find it. It is even more exciting to stand on the same spot where the Civil War photographer stood over 135 years ago and make their historic images. I may have not made history, but I sure was feeling it.

With all the photographs I was taking, I began to think that there are a lot of people, like myself, with an interest in the visual history of the Civil War who would like to see a vivid, color photograph of the same site that the Civil War image was made. Thus, the production of this book in which I have expanded the photographic sites beyond the battlefields to historic buildings, forts, and other locations of the war.

It is amazing that so many of the locations seen in the Civil War photographs are still present today relatively unchanged. Many Civil War battlefields like Gettysburg, and Antietam are preserved as National Historical Military Parks and it is here that so many of the Civil War era photographic locations are preserved. While many of these locations are on public land and accessible, some locations are on private land and do require permission from the owners to visit.

Unfortunately, a different type of battle is being fought over those same battlefields where so many men sacrificed their blood so many years ago. That battle is being fought between those who would turn these hallowed grounds into housing developments, strip malls, race tracts, and amusement parks, and those who would preserve them. Once those grounds are lost they are forever gone to future generations. These locations are our national heritage and every effort should be made to preserve them through such organizations as the Civil War Preservation Trust, National Parks Service, and the National Trust for Historic Preservation.

Photography Information

The majority of the modern day photographs made by the author for this book were made using a Nikon 8008S Auto Focus camera with an AF Nikkor 28–85mm, 1:3.5 – 4.5 zoom lens. The balance of the photographs were made using either the Nikon F3 with the HP viewfinder or the Nikon FE camera with either the Nikon 50mm 1:1.8 or 28 mm 1:2.8 lens. Fill flash, when needed, was accomplished using the Nikon Speedlight SB-20. The majority of images were recorded on Kodak Kodachrome 64, 35 mm slide film and all slide processing was done by Kodak.

Introduction

Civil War photography was made possible because of a series of events that occurred prior the beginning of the war. The development of camera lens optics was made as early as the 1500's, and the chemical process that allowed the optical image made by a camera lens to be captured as a photographic image took place mid-1827. Several years later, in 1839, the photographic process became public.

Most importantly, was the development of a process by which a negative could produce unlimited positive prints. This major advancement in photography was made by an English photographer named Fredrick Scott Archer in 1851, and the process was called wet plate or collodion photography. Glass plates were coated with collodion to make it "sticky" and then covered with a solution of silver nitrate which made it light sensitive. These sensitized glass plates could then be exposed with a light image from the camera lens. Once the image was captured on the glass plates, it could then be developed into a negative image with special chemicals. Following development, the glass plate was fixed, usually with heat, and then coated with a protective, varnish-like material. This final product was a negative much like the negative you would get back, today, with your finished film prints.

Once a glass negative was made prints could be made directly from the image. This was done by passing light through the glass image and then a lens which could then be directed on to a paper coated with a sticky, chicken egg albumin and light sensitive silver nitrate. The exposed paper could then be chemically treated to produce the final image on a glossy, finished, paper. As many prints could be made as the photographer wanted, and, at that time, had great commercial value.

Outdoor photography, during the period between 1861 and 1865, was done with either large view cameras (which utilized glass plates measuring 8 x 10 inches, or more) or the stereographic camera which produced two side-by-side photographic images on a four-by-ten inch glass plate. The photographer in the field had to carry the large and heavy photographic equipment, including dark room supplies, in a horse drawn wagon and because of this four, or more, assistants were required to set up and prepare photographic plates. Later when work was done the equipment had to be loaded onto the wagon and moved to the next location. Look at Sam A. Cooley's photographic team in the photograph on page 9 and see how many assistants are present.

When needed, the colloidal-silver nitrate plates were made on the wagon, in a light protective enclosure, and then carried in a light protective holder to the camera, where it could be exposed. Photographic images were made by focusing the lens image onto (exposing) the sensitized glass plates. The actual exposure was done by removing the cap over the view camera lens and allowing the light, from the scene being photographed, to fall on the sensitized plate. The actual exposure time was from 5 to 10 seconds, or more, depending on the available light. Once the plate was exposed it was placed back into the light protective holder and returned to the wagon enclosure where it was developed.

Adversities such as rain, dust, bumpy roads, heat, cold, insects, supply shortages, sickness, and even war zone dangers, all seemed to conspire against Civil War photographers. Because of these adversities, and other factors such as the chemical quality, temperature, humidity, light conditions, and the experience of the photographer affected the overall quality of the photograph. Also, many glass plates that survived from this period were damaged and prints made from these damaged plates reflected that damage.

Because of these long exposure times anything that moved in the photographic scene would cause a blur in the image. While blurring due to movement may have been disdained by the photographers of the day, blurring of objects like humans, horses, and flags in these photographs suggests movement and imparts a sense of life in an otherwise static scene. Also, the reason humans in these photographs are not smiling is because it was too difficult to hold a smile, without moving, for these long exposure times.

Most of the images produced in the above manner during the Civil War were stereographic images. A special camera with two lenses set apart approximately the same distance as the human's eyes. Two separate images were made simultaneously, each of which was slightly left or right of center. Prints made together from these images were cut and pasted on a card. The card could then be placed in a special apparatus, which made it possible for the viewer to see the images as a single, three-dimensional image. Prints made from these stereographic negatives are different in size and shape than those prints made from the view camera plates.

During the Civil War the public wanted to see these images, but the technology of the day did not allow the mass production in newspapers. What could be done was to convert the glass image to a wood cut, which could then be copied in mass-produced newspapers.

Civil War Images Today

Today, the images produced by Civil War photographers have immense historical value. It has been estimated that over 5,000 images, some of them seen in this book, were produced during this time period. Sadly, many were destroyed and forever lost.

The surviving negatives from these photographers are archived in numerous collections such as the U.S. Army Military History Institute, Library of Congress, National Archives, and numerous private collections.

Now, let's follow these dedicated, heroic photographers and see what those sites, where they created their historic photographs, look like today.

Table of Contents

This book is dedicated to my father-in-law,
Captain Harvey P. Thomas,
a dedicated patriot
and veteran of World War II
and the Korean War.

Civil War photographer Sam A. Cooley's photography wagon and team (right). Note the seven assistants (plus one taking the photo) and the large, view camera at the far right. The sign says "U.S. Photographer, Department of the South". This team was hired by the Northern U.S. government to work in Southern areas, under Union control, recording sites of military interest. Sam Cooley is standing next to the view camera at the far right.

One of Matthew B. Brady's photography teams in the Petersburg, Virginia area, circa 1864 (left). The enclosure where the photographic plates were prepared, and later developed, can be seen in the upper right between the large, rear wheels of the wagon.

Timothy H. O'Sullivan's photography wagon at Manassas, Virginia, July, 1862 (left). After the war, O'Sullivan worked for the government on survey expeditions including the Panama Canal and later traveled west to such areas as Nevada, Utah and California. Later, he returned to Washington D.C and became chief photographer for the United States Treasury.

Alexander Gardner's photography wagon near Fort Riley, Kansas, circa 1867 (right). Following the war Gardner, and his team, traveled West photographing Native Americans and the building of the railroads. Gardner is seated in the middle of the photo and part of a view camera can be seen directly behind him. The assistant is showing Gardner a plant specimen.

George N. Barnard photographing a bridge near Knoxville, Tennessee, circa 1864. (right). Barnard can be seen behind a large view camera at the far right of the photograph. A Federal fort can be seen just to the upper, middle right of the ridge line. Barnard left Brady in 1863 to produce his own work and soon worked for the Northern Military Department. Some of his most famous work was the recording of Sherman's Atlanta Campaign.

Photographer John Moran standing next to his view camera while on assignment in Panama in 1879. (left). This photo demonstrates the size of this type of camera and a sense of what it might weigh.

The engine house at Harper's Ferry, West Virginia circa 1885 (left). It was here at Harper's Ferry, on October 16, 1859, where abolitionist John Brown staged a raid to capture the Federal armory and arsenal. After seizing the armory and arsenal they rounded up many of the town's citizens and held them as hostages hoping that their slaves would join the fight. None of the slaves helped and local militia started to fight back, pinning down Brown and his men. Soon, thereafter, Union troops, under Colonel Robert E. Lee arrived on the scene. By this time Brown and his remaining followers had fled to the engine house so Lee's troops had to storm this structure and in the process killed 10 men and captured the wounded John Brown. Brown was later, in short order, tried, sentenced and hanged. This event may well have been the seminal event that hastened the start of the Civil War. By the time this image was created the structure had become a tourist attraction with the words "John Brown's Fort" written across the doors.

Print depicting U.S. troops under Robert E. Lee's storming the engine house (left).

Engine House at Harper's Ferry, West Virginia today (right). After John Brown's capture this building was called John Brown's Fort and became a tourist attraction. In 1891, the "Fort" was dismantled and moved to Chicago for display. Later, the "Fort" was moved once more to Storer College (located in Camp Hill by Harper's Ferry). In 1968 the "Fort" was returned to Harper's Ferry and was placed 150 feet from its original position. Note in original photograph that the roof top bell tower is missing the bell. Union troops (soldiers of Co. I of the 13th Massachusetts Volunteer Militia) had taken the bell as a souvenir. Today, the bell resides at the John Brown Bell Tower Memorial, Marlborough, Massachusetts.

Abraham Lincoln, and his supporters, at the front of Lincoln's home, celebrating Lincoln's nomination for president, Springfield, Illinois, August, 1860 (right). The home is the only home Abraham Lincoln ever owned and he, and his wife, lived in it for about 17 years before moving to Washington D.C. never to return. Lincoln can be seen standing tall in a white suit, just to the right of the front doorway. Lincoln's wife, Mary, can be seen peeking out of the far left, downstairs, window.

Modern view of Abraham Lincoln's in Springfield, Illinois (left). The home, and the surrounding area, have been restored to their 1860s appearance and are part of the National Park Service. The home is a designated National Historic Site and is open for public tours.

First inauguration of Abraham Lincoln as the 16th president of the United States in front of the U.S. Capitol, March 4, 1861 (above). Lincoln is standing under the canopy at the center of the photograph. Because of the threat of an assassination attempt on Lincoln, sharpshooters were placed in strategic locations on the Capitol to act as deterrence. In part of the inaugural address, Lincoln's made the following statement directed toward the South "I am loth to close. We are not enemies, but friends. We must not be enemies. Though passion may have strained, it must not break our bonds of affection. The mystic chords of memory, stretching from every battle-field, and patriot grave, to every living heart and hearthstone, all over this broad land, will yet swell the chorus of the Union, when again touched, as surely they will be, by the better angels of our nature." A little over a month later (April 12th) Confederate batteries fired on Fort Sumter in Charleston Bay starting the American Civil War.

President Abraham Lincoln's second inauguration in front of the U.S. Capitol, March 4, 1865 (above). Lincoln is seen, hatless, seated to the left of the small podium at the center of the photograph. Directly above Lincoln is a platform with numerous spectators, one of which has been identified as John Wilkes Booth, who later, in 1865, assassinated Lincoln. Directly below Lincoln, according to historians Dorothy and Philip Kunhardt, are five of Booths co-conspirators. Because of the presence of Booth and the co-conspirators, it has been suggested that an assassination attempt of Lincoln was to take place during the inauguration, but for various reasons did not. It was during this inauguration that Lincoln said "With malice toward none, with charity for all" an often quoted statement.

Modern view of the United States Capitol, Washington D.C. and the site of Abraham Lincoln's first and second inauguration (right).

Jefferson Davis being sworn in as President of the Confederacy on the front portico of the Alabama state capitol, Montgomery, Alabama, February 18, 1861 (right). The ceremony is taking place between the two center columns at ground level.

Location where Jefferson Davis was sworn in as President of the Confederacy (above). The bronze star at the base of the right column marks the spot where Davis stood.

Modern view of Jefferson Davis swearing in ceremony location at the Alabama state capitol, Montgomery, Alabama (left).

Fort Johnson, on Morris Island across from Fort Sumter, Charleston Bay, South Carolina. (left). On April 12th, 1861, Fort Johnson was the site of the firing of the first shot on Union held Fort Sumter marking the start of the American Civil War. Following the first shot from this location, batteries ringing Charleston Bay fired a total of 3,341 shells from cannons and mortars before the Union commander of Fort Sumter, Major Robert Anderson, surrendered. Fort Sumter can be seen in the upper left side of the photograph.

Site of Fort Johnson, Morris Island, South Carolina, today (right). Nothing remains of the original fort with only a monument marking the site. The monument reads "At half past four on the morning of April 12, 1861, from a mortar near this spot on Fort Johnson the first shot of the war of secession was fired, by order of Captain George S. James of the Confederate States Army. The Shell exploded above Fort Sumter then occupied by Federal forces thus beginning the tragic conflict which American endured for four years". During the Civil War Fort Sumter was leveled by Union batteries but remained in Confederate hands. Fort Sumter still remains and can be seen through openings in the dense vegetation.

Marshall House in Alexandria, Virginia at the corner of Pitt and King Street (right). On May, 1861, right after Virginia seceded from the Union, Federal troops marched on Alexandria. The Fire Zouaves, led by Colonel Elmer Ellsworth, encountered no resistance. However, upon arriving at this location Ellsworth saw a Confederate flag flying from the flag pole on top of the building. Ellsworth, with several troopers, entered the building, climbed the stairs, and pulled down the flag. Passing down the stairs, Ellsworth was shot, and killed, by innkeeper James Jackson. Jackson, in turn, was immediately killed by a Union soldier. Colonel Ellsworth was the first officer to die in the Civil War and Jackson became a martyr for the Southern cause.

Marshall House location at the southeast corner of Pitt and King Street today (left). After the Ellsworth incident much of the building's interior was ransacked by souvenir hunters. Today, the home has long since been torn down and has been replaced by the Holiday Inn Select. The central location of this hotel makes it an ideal place to stay while in Alexandria.

President Abraham Lincoln's White House, April, 1861 following the fall of Fort Sumter (left). In the center foreground is President Lincoln with his cabinet (most wearing top hats). Surrounding Lincoln and his cabinet are civilian volunteers called the Cassius M. Clay Battalion who were assigned to protect the White House. Mrs. Lincoln can be seen in the upper level, third window from the left.

Modern view of the White House, Washington D.C. (right).

Fort Richardson with the 1st Connecticut Heavy Artillery manning the guns (right). The fort was built in 1861 and was one of a series of forts built south of the Potomac River to protect Washington D.C. The fort was named after Brigadier General Israel B. Richardson of the 2d Michigan Infantry who died in the Battle of Antietam.

The 9th green at the Army and Navy Country Club, Arlington, Virginia today (left). The sand trap and green are at the approximate center of what once was a Civil War fort.

Site of Fort Richardson at the 9th green of the Army and Navy Country Club, Arlington, Virginia today (left). This remaining parapet would have been on the southwest side of the original fort.

Arlington House, or the Custis-Lee Mansion, Arlington, Virginia, circa 1864 (left). This home, built in the early 1800's, was associated with the prominent families of Washington, Custis, and Lee and it was here that Robert E. Lee spent much of his growing up years. When the Civil War broke out, Robert E. Lee sided with the Confederacy and departed. Federal troops confiscated the home and the surrounding grounds were, later, turned into a National Cemetery.

Arlington House, Arlington National Cemetery, Arlington, Virginia today (right). The mansion is called the Lee Mansion National Memorial and is administered by the National Park Service and open to the public. The front porch has a grand view of Washington D.C. across the Potomac.

Centreville, Virginia, March, 1862 with Union soldiers guarding the Braddock Road (right). Centreville, during the Civil War, was a small, rural town near Washington that had seven strategic roads leading into the area, one of which was the Warrenton Turnpike which led directly to Manassas. Because Centreville's location on high ground, and the nearby railroad in Manassas, it occupied a key strategic position (note the high ground at the upper right part of the photograph). During the war this area changed hands five times. The large, dominant building in the upper right was a church (Old Stone Church) which served as a hospital after nearby battles.

Old Stone Church, Centreville Virginia today (left).

Centreville, Virginia today with part of the Old Braddock Road (left). The church itself remains to this day, but is obscured by the thick vegetation at the upper center of the photograph (see different view of church above). This location is just off the Lee Highway (29) and close to Highway 66.

Ruins of the Stone Bridge over Bull Run River, circa 1862 (left). The bridge was part of the Warrenton Turnpike and after the first Battle of Manassas (Battle of Bull Run) in July, 1861, part of the defeated Union forces had to cross back over this bridge in route back to Washington D.C. (from left to right). Later, the bridge was destroyed by Confederate forces.

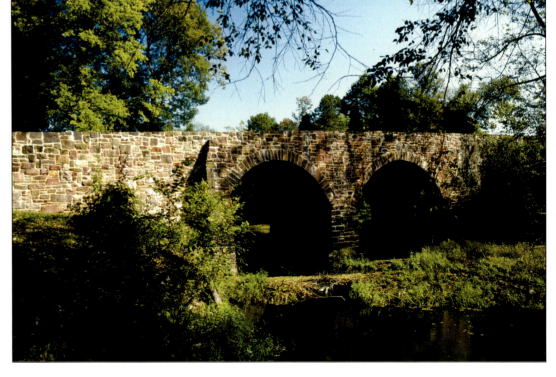

The historic Stone Bridge over Bull Run, Manassas National Battlefield Park, Virginia (right). Because of the heavy growth of vegetation the photograph was taken from a lower location and to the left of the original location. The reconstructed bridge is now maintained by the Park Service and is separate from the Warrenton Turnpike which is directly behind the photographer's position.

Ruins of the Judith Henry home, photographed in March, 1862, following the Battle of Bull Run, or First Battle of Manassas, in July, 1861 (right). During the battle, the home seemed to be the center of the fighting with Mrs. Henry, her son and daughter, and a servant trapped inside. At one point in the battle, Confederate sharpshooters were using the upper floor windows to fire on the Federals. Seeing this, Union artillery was directed toward the house. During this time Mrs. Henry suffered a wound and this, coupled with her poor health, ultimately led to her death. The home itself was severely damaged and later was completely destroyed.

Burial plot for the Henry family. Mrs. Henry is buried in the middle with her son and daughter on each side (left). The land in the background is part of the battlefield over which both battles of Manassas were fought.

Reconstructed Henry Home, Manassas National Military Park today (left). Mrs. Henry's burial plot is behind the left side of the home. The park visitor center is a short walk directly behind the photographer's position.

The Stone House (left) at the junction of the Warrenton turnpike and the Sudley-Manassas Road. During both battles of Manassas, the fighting swirled around this home because of its strategic location at the junction of the major roads in the area.

The historic Stone House, Manassas National Battlefield Park, today (right). This intact and preserved home is one of the most recognizable structures on the battlefield. The Warrenton Turnpike in the foreground (between the wood fences) and the Sudley-Manassas Road off to the left are now heavily trafficked roads.

Dedication of a battle monument honoring the Union after the First Battle of Bull Run, or Manassas, June, 1865 (right). The plaque on the monument reads "In memory of the patriots who fell at Bull Run, July 21, 1861". Judge Abram B. Olin, of the District of Columbia Supreme Court, who delivered dedication speech, is standing next to the rail fence (wearing a tall hat).

First Bull Run Battlefield Monument, Manassas National Military Park, Manassas, Virginia today (left). The monument looks out over the battlefield where so many young soldiers died that day in July, 1861. The tree line in the far background was the location of the Confederate forces just prior to them sweeping across the battlefield (toward the camera's position) and attaining victory.

Pittsburg Landing along the Tennessee River near Corinth, Mississippi several days after the Battle of Shiloh, April, 1862 (left). This landing served as the major supply point for Union troops that had encamped further inland. Union General U.S. Grant's headquarter boat, the Tigress, is seen as the second boat from the right. At one point in the battle, after attacking Confederate troops had completely surprised the Federal forces, upwards of 5,000 frightened Union soldiers had fled to this location.

Pittsburg Landing today at Shiloh National Military Battlefield, Tennessee (right). Little changed since the Civil War battle, this site looks calm, but imagine at the height of the battle, the chaos with ships along the shore unloading fresh troops, terrified soldiers flocking into the area, and the din of artillery and gun fire in the background.

The only known photograph of Confederate troops in a marching order (right). This image was made from the Rosenstock Building in Frederick, Maryland at the corner of Patrick and Market Street looking west. The time was September, 1862 and these troops, possible belonging to General Longstreet's Division, were on their way to Antietam. Note the two Rebel soldiers to the lower left of the Rosenstock sign looking up at the camera. One can only wonder at the fate that awaited these brave, young, men.

Civil War reenactor as a Rebel infantry-man (left).

Location today (left) in the Historical District of Frederick, Maryland near the intersection of Patrick and Market Street (where the truck is turning right) looking west. The original photo of the Confederate troops was taken from across the street where the smaller, white building (Snow White Grill, behind tree in the middle of the photograph) is located. The troops were marching down the street from right to left.

Chatham, or Lacy House, Fredericksburg, Virginia (left). This home's location by the Rappahannock River overlooking the city of Fredericksburg, Virginia made it an ideal location for Union headquarters during the battle of Fredericksburg, December, 1862. From this location, General Edwin V. Sumner, directed the ill-fated attacks against Marye's Heights. In addition, the home served as an artillery and communication center and hospital. Dignitaries such as Abraham Lincoln, Walt Whitman and Clara Barton had visited the home at various times during the war.

Chatham, or Lacy House today (right). Out of view directly to the right, and across the Rappahannock River, is the city of Fredericksburg. The home is now under the care of the Park Service and is open to the public. A small museum is present in the home along with Civil War era displays.

Federal troops massed in Frederick, Maryland on Market Street in front of the Old City Hall, circa 1862 (right). The infantry, on the right side of the street, have been identified as members of the 1st Regiment of the Potomac Home Brigade. In the foreground, on the left side of the street, are members of the Michigan Cavalry. The troops were in Frederick to honor George Washington.

Modern view, at street level, of the Market Street location of massed Federal troops in Frederick, Maryland (left). This location is looking east just past Church Street. The Old City Hall building, with the highest roof line, is on the right side of the photograph. This renovated building now serves as a restaurant.

Confederate dead on the Antietam battlefield with the Dunker Church in the background, September, 19, 1862 (left). The Hagerstown Pike is marked by the wood fencing and can be seen in front of the church. During the battle on September 17, 1862, this area was defended by Confederate forces and was a prime target for advancing (from the right) Union troops. Note the limber chest, the dead horse to the far right, and the shell holes in the church. The church name was derived from the fact that it was of German Baptist origin and the brethren were know as Dunkers.

Modern view of the Confederate dead site and Dunker Church, Antietam National Military Park, Sharpsburg, Maryland (right). The original Dunker Church, one of the most recognizable structures on the battlefield, was destroyed by a storm in 1921. The structure seen today is a reconstruction using the original foundation and bricks. The West Woods, seen in the background of the original photograph, are completely gone. The battlefield museum is located a short distance behind the photographer position.

Confederate soldiers killed in action during the Battle of Antietam, September, 1862 (right). The view is looking north and the bodies lie next to the Hagerstown Pike which is on the other side of wooden fence to the right. The tracks on the left side are part of a farm lane.

Location of dead Confederate soldiers near Hagerstown Pike, Antietam National Military Park, Sharpsburg, Maryland, today (left). The paved road marks the historic Hagerstown Pike.

Burnside's Bridge, Antietam Battlefield, Maryland, September, 1862 (left). During the Battle of Antietam in September, 1862, Union troops under General Ambrose Burnside were to attack the Confederate right flank. Two obstacles were in Burnside's way (1) Antietam Creek and (2) entrenched Confederate troops on the opposite side high ground. A small bridge, that had been built in 1837, made crossing the creek possible. After several gallant attempts by Union troops to storm across the bridge they were finally able to drive the Rebel soldiers from the high ground. Once the bridge and high ground was secured, thousands of Federal troops were able to cross the bridge and attack the Confederate right flank. The cost was high with approximately 500 Federal soldiers killed or wounded in this effort. After the battle the bridge was called Burnside's Bridge.

View of Burnside's Bridge from the Confederate high ground (above).

Burnside's Bridge, Antietam National Military Park, Sharpsburg, Maryland today (right). The bridge has been maintained in its original, Civil War era, condition. Note the high ground on the opposite side where the Rebel troops had a clear, downward angle to shoot at the Union troops attempting to cross the bridge.

View of the Battlefield of Antietam, September 17, 1862. This location was close to the Pry House, which served as the head-quarters for Union General McClellan during the battle. The man at the lower right appears to be looking through his field glasses toward the battle area which was at least one mile away. Union artillery units can be seen at the left side, and Union soldiers can be seen on the right side.

Battlefield view location today, near Sharpsburg, Maryland (left). This location lies on private grounds and appears unchanged when compared to the Civil War era photograph. The Pry Home, which still exits today, is about a quarter of a mile away to the right-rear of this photographic site.

Union battery that fought during the Battle of Antietam, September, 1862 (left). This location is looking north over fields where Federal and Rebel troops were engaged in fighting a few days earlier (note the dead horse at the left center). The infamous "Bloody Cornfield" where Union and Rebel troops fought back and forth during the earlier stages of the battle can be seen can be seen just below the tree line at the center of the photograph.

Union battery location at Antietam National Military Park, Sharpsburg, Maryland today (right). The "Bloody Cornfield" can be seen as the brownish patch at the upper, right just behind the small, bare tree. During the initial stages of the Battle of Antietam, part of the Union attack started from a location at the far tree line at the upper right, and moved toward this location which, at that time, was held by Confederate forces.

Dead Confederate soldiers in "Bloody Lane", following the Battle of Antietam, September, 19, 1862 (right). From this sunken road, rebel troops poured a devastating fire in the ranks of advancing Union troops. After numerous charges on this position, and after suffering staggering amounts of casualties, the Union troops were able to break through the sunken road defense at a bend in the line. From this point the Union troops were able to enfilade the sunken road lined with rebel troops, extracting a measure of revenge. The surviving Confederate forces pulled back to a new defensive position leaving behind their dead. The sunken road later became known as the Bloody Lane.

Modern view of the Bloody Lane at Antietam National Military Park, Sharpsburg, Maryland (left). The original sunken road has been preserved in its entirety and appears much as it did during that fateful battle. An elevated observation tower has been built at the upper part of the road (out of the photo to the upper, left) which affords a spectacular view of not only the sunken road, but most of the battlefield.

Grave of a Union officer and an unburied Confederate soldier, Antietam battlefield, September, 19, 1862 (left). Note the small grave marker on the mounded grave site. This location was on Miller's farm fields between the "Bloody Cornfield" and the Smoketown Road and Dunker Church and is where, just two days earlier, Union and Confederate forces were engaged in battle. (For more detail concerning this location and the identity of the dead Union officer please refer to William Frassanito's book "Antietam".

Modern view of dead Union officer's grave site on Millers farm, Antietam National Military Park, Sharpsburg, Maryland (right). The body of the Union officer was disinterred and now rests in Woodlawn Cemetery, Monroe Michigan. The body of the dead Confederate soldier remains unknown. This part of the battlefield is on a private farm just north of the Smoketown Road and at various time of the year the fields will be covered with farm crops.

Union burial detail, with Union dead, following the Battle of Antietam, September 19, 1862 (right). Following the Confederate's abandonment of the battlefield after the battle Union burial details were left with the grisly task of gathering, and burying, the dead which were strewn across the battlefield. This view is looking northwest toward the North Woods on the Miller farm fields. The Hagerstown Pike is to the right and out of view.

Union burial detail location, Antietam National Military Park, Sharpsburg, Maryland today (left). Today, this location is on an active, privately owned, farm but can be easily seen from the Hagerstown Pike.

Sharpsburg, Maryland, September 22, 1862 after the battle of Antietam (left). The view is looking northwest down Hall Street with part of the Antietam Battlefield visible in the far background. The building seen just above, and to the left, of the large house in the center of the photograph is the Saint Paul's Episcopal Church. The photographer's wagon (Alexander Gardner) can be seen on the street in the foreground.

Modern view of Hall Street and part of Sharpsburg, Maryland (right). Parts of the present day Antietam National Military Park can be seen in the far background. The old Saint Paul's Episcopal Church building has since been replaced by a newer structure.

President Abraham Lincoln meeting with General McClellan and staff on October 3, 1862 following the Battle of Antietam in September, 1862 (right). This meeting took place at the head-quarters of General Fitz-John Porter who was using the home of Stephen Grove just outside the town of Sharpsburg, Maryland. General McClellan is the fourth person to Lincoln's right. The man standing to the far right, by the tent, is Captain George A. Custer. Custer, early in his Army career, was serving as a McClellan staff aide.

The President Lincoln-General McClellan meeting site outside of the city Sharpsburg, Maryland today (left). While the Antietam Battlefield is within a National Military Park and is open to the public, this home is privately owned and permission from the owner is necessary to visit. However, this site can be viewed from the Shepherdstown Road on the west side of Sharpsburg.

Fairfax Courthouse, Fairfax, Virginia, June, 1863 (left). The cavalrymen in the left foreground were part of a Union force that was maintaining a position between General Robert E. Lee's forces as they moved north, and Washington D.C. In June, 1861, Confederate and Union troops skirmished at this location. During the battle, Captain John Q. Marr of the 17th VA. Infantry was killed. Capt. Marr was the first Confederate officer killed in the war. In March, 1863, in a daring early morning raid, Confederate Captain John Mosby and his band of partisan rangers, rode into the Fairfax Court House area and captured 30 Union soldiers including Union General Edwin Stroughton.

Fairfax Courthouse, Fairfax, Virginia, today (right). This building, listed in the National Register of Historic Places, was built in 1800 and during the Civil War was occupied by Union troops. While the courthouse itself is intact, building additions have blocked out the view of the some of the original courthouse building.

Union breastworks on Little Round Top after the Battle of Gettysburg, July, 1863 (right). The view is from the Union side of the rock breastwork and is at the crest of Little Round Top. Only a few days prior to this image being made, Federal troops from Michigan and New York, were in a desperate struggle with Rebel soldiers trying to capture this location.

Modern view of the Union breastworks location on Little Round Top, Gettysburg National Military Park, Gettysburg, Pennsylvania (left).

Confederate dead at the base of Little Round Top following the Battle of Gettysburg, July, 1863 (left). The photograph was taken a few days after the end of the battle. The dead soldiers lie next to a small stream called Plum Run which was also called "Bloody Run" because it was said to have run red with the blood spilled on the battlefield.

Plum Run at the base of Little Round Top, Gettysburg National Military Park today (right). Confederate forces were unable to dislodge Union defenders from this critical location (Little Round Top) which helped prevent a Rebel victory during this historic battle. Part of Little Round Top can be seen at the upper right part of the photograph. The park service has kept vegetation cleared from this site so that viewers can visualize what it looked like after the battle.

Confederate dead after the Battle of Gettysburg, July, 1863 (right). The location was at the edge of the Rose Woods where fighting took place on July 2, 1863. Burial details were in the process of collecting the bodies for temporary burial when the photographer, Alexander Gardner, arrived to take the image. Note the photographer's wagon at top.

Modern view of the Confederate dead location in the Gettysburg National Military Park today (left). The large rock, at the upper right, can be used as an identification marker. The small trees growing in the foreground are in the approximate positions were the Rebel soldier's bodies were lying over 140 years ago.

Confederate soldiers captured by Union troops during, or after, the Battle of Gettysburg, July, 1863 (left). What is so good about this image is the detail of the typical, Rebel infantryman. This location is next to the Lutheran Theological Seminary on Seminary Ridge, Gettysburg, Pennsylvania. The wood logs seen in the picture were part of a protective breastworks used by the Rebel troops during the initial stages of the battle.

Modern day Civil War reenactor as a Rebel soldier (left).

Modern view of Seminary Ridge location where Rebel prisoners once stood today (right). Part of Cemetery Hill is visible to the upper left background and the Lutheran Seminary is just out of view to the right. The wood fence present in the 1863 view has been replaced by the stone wall.

Union General George Mead's headquarters on Cemetery Hill following the Battle of Gettysburg, July, 1863 (right). General Meade was the commander of the Army of the Potomac at the time of the Gettysburg battle and was responsible for the successful defense that prevented a potential defeat at the hands of the Confederate army commanded by Robert E. Lee. The headquarter building used by Meade at Gettysburg is the small building (a local civilian's farmhouse) seen at the upper center part of the photograph. This area received heavy bombardment from Rebel artillery preceding Pickett's charge on July 3, 1863. Note the dead horse lying on the Tanneytown Road.

Present day view of Mead's Headquarters and Tanneytown Road, Gettysburg National Military Park, Gettysburg, Pennsylvania (left). The site of Pickett's charge on the last day of the Battle of Gettysburg, and the present day Gettysburg Visitor Center, is out of view to the left side of this photograph.

The Lutheran Theological Seminary following the Battle of Gettysburg, Pennsylvania, July, 1863 (left). Mathew Brady's photographic team took this picture, with one of the assistants (or Brady himself?) sitting on the fence, about two weeks after the battle. At this time the Seminary was being used as a hospital. During the battle, the cupola at the top was an ideal observation post and was used by both sides as this area changed hands. When Confederate troops controlled this part of the battlefield, General Robert E. Lee made several visits to the cupola.

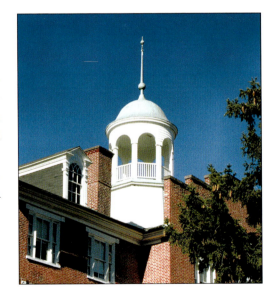

Cupola on top of the Lutheran Theological Seminary, Gettysburg, Pennsylvania today (right).

The Lutheran Theological Seminary, Gettysburg National Military Park, Gettysburg, Pennsylvania today (right).

Confederate General Robert E. Lee's headquarters during the Battle of Gettysburg, July, 1863 (right). The home, built around 1830, belonged to Widow Mary Thompson and one of the two figures in front of the house may be Mrs. Thompson. Because of its location at the crest of Seminary Ridge, Lee used this site after Union forces were pushed back on the first day of the battle. The road in the fore-ground is the Chambersburg Pike and it leads into the town of Gettysburg to the right.

General Robert E. Lee's headquarters, Gettysburg National Military Park today (left). The building is now called the Lee's Headquarter Museum and contains an excellent collection of Civil War memorabilia from that momentous battle.

Union breastworks on Culp's Hill following the Battle of Gettysburg (left). This photograph, taken on July 15, 1863 almost two weeks after the battle, clearly shows the breastworks of rocks, logs, and dirt put up by New York Regiments to protect them from Confederate assaults up the hill to the left. Two of Brady's assistants are seated on a rock.

Modern view of breastwork location on Culp's Hill, Gettysburg National Military Park, Pennsylvania (right). Little is left of the breastworks except for low mounded earth running from the lower left of the photograph to the upper, right center. The rock that Brady's assistants sat on is still visible at the right center between the two larger trees. A field monument marking the New York regiments location is just visible in the upper right behind the large tree.

President Abraham's procession on the way to Gettysburg Soldiers National Cemetery, Gettysburg, Pennsylvania, November 19, 1863 (right). The procession is traveling toward the camera on Baltimore Street and is making a slight, right turn onto Emmitsburg Road. The marching Union soldier's rifle bayonets can be seen gleaming in the sun. Several images were recorded at this location, and at least one shows what appears to be Lincoln himself riding a horse. A short time later President Lincoln gave his famous Gettysburg address.

Saddle on Lincoln's horse during the procession from downtown Gettysburg to the cemetery (above). The saddle is on display at the Gettysburg museum.

Modern view of Lincoln's procession route on Baltimore Street, Gettysburg, Pennsylvania (left). The overhanging stop lights at the center of the photo marks the intersections of Emmitsburg Road and Baltimore Street. A Holiday Inn is located to right (overhang) and the Jennie Wade (the only civilian to be killed during the battle) home is to the immediate right, rear of this location.

Two views of the dedication ceremonies at Soldier's National Cemetery, Gettysburg, Pennsylvania, November 19, 1863 (above). It was during this ceremony that President Abraham Lincoln gave his famous Gettysburg address. The speaker's platform is seen as a slight rise in the upper, right and slightly to the left of the tent on the left photo. Detailed examination of the right photo has revealed what appears to be a seated hatless Lincoln (upper left part of photo).

Site of Lincoln's Gettysburg address, Soldiers National Cemetery, Gettysburg, Pennsylvania today (right). The dominant Soldiers National Monument was dedicated in 1869 and marks an approximate site of the speaker's platform (the actual site may have been more to the right and rear of the monument). For a more detailed analysis of the exact location of the speaker's platform see William Frassanito's "Early Photography at Gettysburg".

Courthouse in Murfreesboro, Tennessee, circa 1863 (right). Murfreesboro became a major supply area for the Union because of its proximity to the Nashville & Chattanooga railroad. Men of the 9th Michigan were guarding this location in July, 1862, when they came under attack by Nathan B. Forest's Rebel horseman. The Federals quickly made a fortress of the courthouse, but later had to surrender.

Courthouse in Murfreesboro, Tennessee today (left). This location is in the center of town and a short distance away from the Stone River Battlefield National Park, where the South suffered defeat in December, 1862.

Wounded Union soldiers at the John Marye home, Fredericksburg, Virginia, 1864 (left). These soldiers had been wounded in the Battle of the Wilderness and Spotsylvania, May 1864 and are seen recuperating next to the Marye home. The photographer had made two images of the wounded at this location. In addition to this scene, the camera was turned around 180 degrees and wounded gathered under a large tree were photographed. Of the two scenes, the wounded under the tree (see next) was widely used in books, calendars and even TV documentaries.

Marye House, Fredericksburg, Virginia today (right). This building is now part of the Mary Washington College and is a short walk from the Fredericksburg Battlefield Museum.

Wounded Union soldiers recuperating at the Marye Home, Fredericksburg, Virginia (left). The photo was taken in 1864 and the wounded soldiers were from General U.S. Grant's Campaign in the Wilderness and Spotsylvania. The man standing at the far left is a medical officer. At the start of the war, the Marye home belonged to the lieutenant governor of Virginia. The location of this home on the heights above Fredericksburg made it a key Confederate site during the Union's ill-fated loss in the Battle of Fredericksburg, December, 1862. Later in the war this area was captured by Federal forces and the Marye home was turned into a Union hospital.

Grounds around the Marye home, Fredericksburg, Virginia today (left). Note that the tree in the original photograph still stands. The ground around the Marye home, and the home itself, has been preserved in their original state and is easily accessible.

The Wall at Marye's Heights, Fredericksburg, Virginia, circa 1863 (left). These Rebel soldiers were killed during the Battle of Chancellorsville, when Federal troops successfully stormed the wall and drove the defenders out. This is part of the same wall behind which Confederate soldiers poured a devastating fire into advancing Union troops during the First Battle of Fredericksburg. In that earlier engagement, 7,000 Union soldiers and officers were lost in a futile attempt to gain this ground.

Remnants of the original wall at the Fredericksburg National Military Park (left).

The Wall at Marye's Heights, Fredericksburg and Spotsylvania National Military Park, Virginia today (right). The wall seen in this photograph is a replica of the original wall, only a small part of which has been preserved at a different site (see above).

Camp of the 44th New York overlooking Alexandria, Virginia, March, 1864 (right). The 44th New York was also known as the "Peoples Ellsworth Regiment" in honor of Colonel Elmer Ellsworth who was killed by a Southern sympathizer in the Marshall House Hotel (see Marshall House, page 17). This photograph is unique in that it is part of a four plate series which, when put together, displays a panoramic view of not only a Union soldier encampment, but also of Civil War era Alexandria, Virginia. King Street, which runs into the heart of Alexandria, is seen at the left center. The 44th New York fought with distinction in the Peninsula campaign, Second Bull Run, Fredericksburg, Gettysburg, the Wilderness and Cold Harbor.

Modern view of the 44th New York encampment site, Alexandria, Virginia (left). This site is now part of the Masonic Temple grounds and is open to the public. King Street can still be seen as the tree lined street at left center.

Andersonville Prison, a Confederate prison for Union prisoners of war, Georgia, circa 1863 (left). The photograph was taken from the stockade wall looking down at the center of the prison grounds. A small stream, which ran through the center of the prison, was used both as a latrine and a source of water for drinking and bathing. Needless to say, the death rate from such diseases as typhoid fever was high. It was estimated that at one time the prison covered 26 acres with up to 32,899 Union prisoners and a death rate from disease and starvation as high as 3,000 per month. The commandant for the prison, Henry Wirtz, was hanged at Old Capitol Prison in Washington D.C. after the war ended. (See Old Capitol Prison, page 85).

Andersonville Prison, Georgia today (right). The white posts to the far right mark the stockade wall location with the inside posts marking what was then called the dead line. If a prisoner went beyond the dead line posts he would be shot by Rebel guards. A partially re-constructed stockade wall can be seen at the left center just below the tree line. It was here where the North entrance was located and where new prisoners entered the grounds for the first time.

Andersonville Prison, a Confederate prison for Union soldiers of war, Georgia, circa 1863 (right). The photograph was taken from the stockade wall and dramatically shows the crowded conditions. All prisoners had to fend for themselves for shelter. Some were able to build small lean-to structures which provided some protection against the heat, rain, and cold. Otherwise, the soldiers simply camped out in the open on bare ground.

Interior grounds of Andersonville Prison by the reconstructed north gate, Georgia today (left). Various types' shelters have been built by the park service to demonstrate the living conditions that the soldiers had to endure. The partially reconstructed stockade wall in the background has a guard tower (upper right) from which the Rebel guard could look down on the prisoners. The posts below the stockade wall marked the dead line, a point beyond which the prisoners must not go under threat of being shot by the guard. Soldiers who could no longer endure the unbearable conditions were said to have walked into the area between the dead line and stockade wall just to be shot, a form of suicide.

Ruins of Fort Desperate, a Confederate stronghold at Port Hudson, Louisiana, circa 1863 (left). Some 295 Confederate officers and men built, and defended, this location against the Union siege of Port Hudson which lasted 48 days. This is considered the longest, true siege, in American History. Control of this location on the Mississippi River was of the utmost importance to both sides, but the Union eventually prevailed. The destruction seen in this photograph speaks for the severe fighting that took place.

Modern view of Fort Desperate, Port Hudson State Historic Park, Louisiana (right). This site is a National Historical Landmark and is open to the public It is located off US Highway 61 at 756 West Plains-Port Hudson Road in Zachary, Louisiana (north of Baton Rouge).

Union General U.S. Grant and his staff on Lookout Mountain, Chattanooga, Tennessee, circa 1863 (right). General Grant is at the far left with a cigar in his mouth. This photograph was taken after the Union victory on Lookout Mountain and Missionary Ridge (Battle of Chattanooga). It is interesting that Grant chose this location to have his photograph taken as the more stunning Lookout Mountain overview, where so many officers and men had their image recorded (see page 61), is at the middle, far background behind the small building (Royan Linn's photograph studio).

Grant photo location during the summer months showing the dense vegetation making it difficult to identify (left). Part of a steep stair case, which can be used to access paths below Point Lookout, can be seen at the lower right.

General U.S. Grant photograph location on Lookout Mountain, Tennessee (left). This location is a short walk down the path to the right behind Point Lookout and the Ochs Memorial (upper, right background). Many of the rock formations seen in the original photo's can be seen in this modern photo.

Pulpit Rock on Lookout Mountain, Chattanooga, Tennessee, 1864 (left). The photo shows a tripod signal (upper left side) that had been erected by officers of the U.S. Coast survey. Before Union troops captured this location during the Battle of Lookout Mountain, November, 1863, Jefferson Davis, President of the Confederacy, gave an inspirational speech to Stevenson's division from the location. The term pulpit rock was coined and later Union troops changed the name to Devil's Pulpit.

Modern view of Pulpit Rock, Lookout Mountain and Point Park, Chattanooga, Tennessee (right). Pulpit Rock is somewhat difficult to find because it is off the park paths and surrounded by dense vegetation. It is about 500 yards behind the Ochs Memorial location. Point Park is a Civil War site well worth visiting with its spectacular views of Chattanooga, a museum located near the park grounds, and (during the summer months) reenactors are present with historical information and demonstrations.

Portraits of Union soldiers and officers on Lookout Mountain, Chattanooga, Tennessee (left). Following the Union victories at Lookout Mountain and Missionary Ridge (The Battles for Chattanooga) in November, 1863, a studio was set up on this spectacular outcropping by an enterprising photographer named Royan M. Linn where everybody from generals to infantryman paid to have their image recorded.

Cavalryman (see front cover), possible of the Pennsylvania 9th Regiment (above).

General Joseph Hooker, commander of forces that captured Lookout Mountain, sits for his photograph (left).

Major General D.C. McCallum on the right and an unidentified officer (right). At the end of the Civil War, McCallum had become the Director and General Manager of the Military Railroad of the U.S.

Point Lookout on Lookout Mountain, Chattanooga, Tennessee today (above). The Tennessee River is visible in the upper part of the photograph and the city of Chattanooga is out of the field of view to the right. A memorial called the Ochs Memorial now resides where the Linn studio once stood and offers a small museum and the still spectacular view.

Behind the Union lines during the siege of Vicksburg, Mississippi, circa 1863 (left). The soldiers seen in the photograph are from the 45th Illinois Infantry, and because of the prolonged siege they fashioned dugouts in the side of the hill to protect them against the elements and Confederate bombardment. The home at the upper right was owned by James and Adeline Shirley. During the initial stages of the battle, the Shirley family was caught in the crossfire and had to be evacuated to safety by Union soldiers. The home itself survived destruction and remains today within the Vicksburg National Military Park.

Shirley House today (above).

Site of Union siege line, and Shirley House, Vicksburg National Military Park today (right). Most of the slope where Union soldiers had made their dugouts has been filled, but part of the slope still remains beyond the trees at the far right. The Shirley house is the only wartime structure remaining within the park.

U.S.S. Cairo, ironclad gunboat on the Mississippi River, circa 1861 (right). This gunboat had 14 mounted cannons, of various sizes, on all sides of the boat and seventeen officers and 158 enlisted men. The Cairo operated on the Mississippi and Tennessee River and was involved in several engagements with Confederate warships. On December 12, 1862, while operating on the Yazoo River north of Vicksburg, Mississippi, the Cairo struck a Confederate torpedo (underwater mine) and sunk in 12 minutes with no loss of life.

U.S.S. Cairo, Vicksburg National Military Park, Vicksburg, Mississippi today (left). In the summer of 1956 the Cairo was discovered by Edwin C. Bearss, and in 1960 the recovery process started. By 1965 the Cairo was, in parts, on dry land. In 1977 the U.S.S. Cairo was transported to its permanent resting spot, under a protective covering, at the Vicksburg National Cemetery. A museum is present with and excellent collection of recovered Cairo artifacts. The curve fence encloses that part of the boat where the torpedo caused the fatal damage.

Spotsylvania Battlefield, near the "Bloody Angle", May 12, 1864 (left). This Alfred Waud drawing depicts Union troops crouched in trenches exchanging gunfire with Confederate troops just yards away. In some places, along the line, the fighting was hand to hand across the breastworks. A Union combatant wrote "Our men would reach over the logs and fire into the faces of the enemy, would stab over with their bayonets: many were shot and stabbed through crevices and holes between the logs". Alfred Waud, preeminent Civil War combat artist, made many of his drawings at the site of action during the actual battle.

A testament to the intense battle at the "Bloody Angle" is this 22 inch diameter tree trunk (left) that was standing just behind the Rebel lines being felled by concentrated Union musket fire. The tree was removed from the battlefield and now resides in the Smithsonian Museum, Washington D.C.

Battle line near the "Bloody Angle" at Spotsylvania National Military Park, today (right). The earthworks can still be seen running up the middle of the picture. A monument can be seen at the far, upper middle of the picture, which marks the point where the battle line makes a turn forming an angle. It was here, at the angle, where some of the fiercest fighting took place resulting in the name "Bloody Angle"

Massaponax Church, Virginia, May 21, 1864 (right). During the Spotsylvania campaign, Union Generals Grant and Meade were moving their troops around the flank of Confederate General Robert E. Lee's forces. General Grant used this church as a temporary headquarters and it was here that photographer Timothy H. O'Sullivan had the good fortune to make a series of photographs showing General Grant, and his staff, in the process of making war plans and writing dispatches.

Massaponax Baptist Church, Virginia today (left). This church is active today and the building has been completely preserved. It's location is south of Fredericksburg off Telegraph Road (Highway 1) which runs parallel to Highway 95 and east of the Spotsylvania Court House.

Union General U.S. Grant and staff in front of the Massaponax Church, May 21, 1865 (left). This meeting occurred during Grant's Spotsylvania campaign against Robert E. Lee's forces. Grant is seen with his legs crossed directly underneath the tree. To Grant's right, at the end of the next pew over, is General Meade with his slouch hat. To Grant's immediate left is Charles Dana, Assistant Secretary of War and to Dana's left is General Rawling, Grant's chief of staff. The photograph was taken from inside the church looking out the upper window.

Massaponax Baptist Church location of Grants meeting. Because entrance to the church was not available, the photograph was taken outside, and directly underneath the window used by O'Sullivan to take the historic photograph.

Union Battery position with mortar on the Petersburg siege lines, Petersburg, Virginia, September, 1864. (right). A 13 inch mortar, mortar shells, and crew are seen at the right center and a protective bombproof at the left, center. The mortar was delivered to this location on specially built railroad tracks and railroad car platform which can be seen to the far, center right. The upward angle of the mortar would seem to indicate the Rebel line was not far away over the hill in the background.

Civil War mortar and shells on display at Battery Park, Charleston, South Carolina (above).

13 inch mortar position, Petersburg National Military Park, Petersburg, Virginia today (left). Because of the dense vegetation, the camera angle is further to the left than the original. A replica mortar can be seen in the original position at the extreme, right center, and the bombproof at the left center. The original mortar was referred to as the "dictator" and, today, is either mounted at the front of the Connecticut State Capitol or on the grounds of Fort McNair, Washington D.C.

The Crater, Petersburg Battlefield, Virginia, circa 1865 (left). In an attempt to break through the Confederate lines during the siege of Petersburg, Union troops (more specifically those with mining experience), dug a tunnel to a point under the Rebel line and placed explosives. On July 30, 1864 the explosives were detonated killing numerous Rebel soldiers and creating a huge crater in the line. Union troops rushed into the crater to attempt a breakthrough, but were met with a stout defense by Rebel troops. Because of poor communications and planning on the part of the Union commanders a breakthrough was not realized and in the end Union troops suffered more casualties than the Southern forces.

The Crater at Petersburg National Military Park, Virginia today (right). The original blast created a hole 200 feet long, 50 feet wide and 30 feet deep. Remnants of the present day crater are seen as erosion and plant growth have partially filled the blast hole. A depiction of the Battle of the Crater can be seen in the movie "Cold Mountain" released in 2003.

Union Battery in a captured Confederate Battery on the eastern front of the Petersburg, Virginia siege line, June, 1864 (right). Brady's photographic team recorded this image and Brady, with a straw hat, can be seen at the far, center left. A few days after this photo was taken the 1st Connecticut Heavy Artillery took over this position. The 1st Connecticut came from Fort Richardson which was involved in the defenses of Washington D.C. (see page 19).

Union Battery location, Petersburg National Military Park and Battlefield, Petersburg, Virginia today (left). This location, referred to as Battery 5, still has major portions of the preserved earthworks which can be seen from left center to right center.

Union Battery during the siege of Petersburg, June, 1864 (left). This photograph was taken by Brady's photographic team and Brady has placed himself, quite conspicuously, near the cannon at the center. It was suggested that this photograph was taken during the heat of battle, but careful examination reveals that it was staged. Because of the long exposure times required by view cameras of the day (see Introduction) the hurried movements of artillery units during actual battle would have caused extensive blurring. Note that most, if not all, figures in the photo are in focus, and not blurred, indicating that they held their position for several seconds. Further, note the blurring of the flag at the upper left as it was being whipped about by the wind. Also, note the rather casual attitude of some of the men, like those at the lower right, which suggest that they were not under fire from enemy batteries. One thing for sure, this picture does afford one of the better views of Matthew Brady himself with his characteristic straw hat.

Union battery and Brady's photographic location, Petersburg National Military Park, Petersburg, Virginia today (right). A park road in the foreground cuts through this former Union battery and right over the spot where Brady once stood. Only a placard, seen at the far left by the tree, identifies the Union battery position where a Union artillery crew posed for Brady's camera over 140 years ago.

Former Confederate fort on the outskirts of Atlanta, Georgia, 1865 (right). The Confederate forces abandoned Atlanta in 1864 under pressure from Union General William Tecumseh Sherman's Federal troops. This image was made looking south down Peachtree Street toward Atlanta. The tents seen in the background belonged to Union troops.

Confederate fort location today looking south down Peachtree Street at the intersection with Third Avenue, Atlanta, Georgia (left). Third Street is the cross street at the overhanging street light.

Interior view of Fort McAllister on the Great Ogeechee River, Georgia, December, 1864 (left). Fort McAllister was a Confederate, earthen fort with heavy artillery which protected the city of Savannah, Georgia from Union invasion by way of the Ogeechee River. On December 13, 1864, Union General Tecumseh Sherman's troops captured this fort by land invasion (and Savannah, Georgia 8 days later). Following the fort's capture, all artillery pieces were dismantled and removed. Note the wooden carriage, minus its cannon, at the lower right center.

Interior of Fort McAllister State Park, Richmond Hill, Georgia today (right). Fort McAllister is one of the best preserved examples of earthen forts in the United States. Prior to the advent of rifled cannons, the military built brick forts (see Fort Pulaski, page 74) to protect important locations. Rifled cannons with their long range, accuracy, and destructive power, made brick forts obsolete. To neutralize rifled cannons, forts made of mounded earth (bombproof) to protect vital points were devised and proved to be highly effective. Union gunboats tried, on several occasions, to destroy Fort McAllister, but were unsuccessful.

Confederate gun at Fort McAllister on the Great Ogeechee River, Georgia, 1864 (right). The artillery piece appears to be a Parrott Rifle on a wood carriage. After the capture of this fort all artillery was dismantled and moved to another fort near Savannah.

Gun emplacement at Fort McAllister State Park, Richmond Hill, Georgia, today (left). The artillery piece appears to be a reproduction, or a Civil War era Columbiad, on a wood carriage. The park is a combination historic site and camping area with a history museum and can be reached by traveling west out of Savannah, Georgia on I-90 about 6 miles to exit 90. Follow the signs to the park (about 4 miles.).

Interior view of Fort Pulaski, near Savannah, Georgia, showing the damaged rear parapet following Union bombardment (left). This fort was a brick and mortar fort built on the Savannah River to guard Savannah, Georgia. During the Civil War it was thought that this fort was impregnable to bombardment from Union attacks. However, that was before the advent of the accurate and destructive capability of the rifled cannons. Starting on April 10, 1862, Union land based batteries with 9 inch Columbiads and rifled cannons, opened up on the fort, and within one day's bombardment, and a total of over 5,000 shells, the Confederate forces surrendered (April 11, 1862). During the bombardment, shells had come close to blowing up the magazine and had that occurred the detonation would have killed, or wounded, every person inside the fort. The photograph shows large wood beams and dirt laid at an angle on the backside of the fort to deflect incoming shells. Note the shell damage to the exposed brick and mortar.

Modern view of the inside parade grounds and back side of Fort Pulaski National Monument, Savannah, Georgia (right). The fort was built on Cockspur Island between the years of 1829 and 1847 using slave labor. Today, this preserved, five-sided brick and mortar fort can be reached by driving a short distance east out of Savannah on Highway 80 or on Islands Expressway which meets with Highway 80.

Main entrance to Fort Delaware circa 1865 (left). The fort, originally built to protect the ports of Wilmington and Philadelphia, is situated on Pea Patch Island in the middle of the Delaware River, south of Wilmington, Delaware. After the Civil War started, the fort was turned into a Union prison for Confederate prisoners. Between 1862 and 1865 a total of 33,000 Rebel prisoners were incarcerated at this site and of these, 2,700 died from various causes. Most of the prisoners that died at this site were buried at Finn's Point directly across the river on the New Jersey side. Political prisoners were housed inside the fort walls while other prisoners of war were confined in barracks built in open areas outside of the fort.

Monument at Finn's Point burial site for Confederate soldiers who died at Fort Delaware prison. (left).

Civil War reenactor portraying a political prisoner inside the walls of Fort Delaware (right).

Main entrance to Fort Delaware today (right). The fort is maintained as a State Park and is open to the public (closed during the winter months). Visitors can take a short ferry ride from Delaware City to Pea Patch Island and reenactors are often present to answer your questions and give demonstrations. A book store is present in one of the fort's rooms. Except for the fort itself, few of the original prison structures remain and natural vegetation has been allowed to grow back where the prisoner barracks were once located. For hikers, well maintained trails are present throughout the former prison grounds.

Two interior views of Fort Fisher, North Carolina following its capture by Union forces (above). This fort was a Confederate earthen fort which guarded the important Southern port of Wilmington, North Carolina and prevented Union Naval attacks up the Cape Fear River. On January 12, 1865, the fort was bombarded by both Federal ships and by land based batteries. The bombardment was followed by an assault of more than 3,300 Union infantry. On January 15, 1865, the fort was captured by the Union. The images show some cannons still in place and bombproof openings at the base of the earthen mounds. Once the Union troops breached the defensive line, mound to mound and bombproof to bombproof fighting ensued before those Rebels not killed, wounded, or captured, fled down the peninsula to Battery Buchanan (see page 78), where they later surrendered.

Interior view of Fort Fisher today (right). This location is part of the Fort Fisher State Recreation Area. and only a small portion of the original fort remains. Fortunately, some important locations during the original battle, including the site where Union troops broke through the defensive line (just out of view to the left of this image), have been preserved. This area is about 18 miles south of Wilmington, North Carolina and can be reached by driving south out of Wilmington on Highway 421 which joins Highway 132.

Print depicting Union infantry attacking the heavily fortified earthen Fort Fisher held by Confederate forces, January 15, 1865 (right). Following an intense bombardment by Federal Naval gunboats and land cannons, the infantry attacked the fortifications at several points. The location depicted in this print was where Federal troops were able to make a break through. This break through ultimately lead to a Union Victory and soon thereafter Union forces were able to capture the important Confederate sea port of Wilmington, North Carolina.

Modern view of the Union breakthrough location at Fort Fisher (Fort Fisher State Recreation Area) today (left). From this position the Atlantic Ocean at the upper left side (barely visible) and the Cape Fear River at the right side out of view. The earthen mounds seen in this image are all that is left of the original fort.

Battery Buchanan, tip of Federal Point, North Carolina, circa 1865 (right). When in Confederate hands, this battery bristled with artillery to help protect Wilmington, North Carolina from Union gun boats sailing up Cape Fear River. This battery was also located about a mile southwest from Fort Fisher. When Union forces attacked Fort Fisher in Jan. 1865, Confederate troops fled to this location and later surrendered.

Battery Buchanan, Federal Point, North Carolina today (left). Only the vegetation growing on this historic site is keeping it from completely eroding away. This location is south of Wilmington, North Carolina on Route 421 between the Cape Fear River, and the Atlantic Ocean and about one mile beyond the larger Fort Fisher remains.

Falls Church, Virginia (right). This church was erected in 1769 with George Washington an appointed church warden. The building has changed little since being built and is at the intersection of the historic Lee Highway and Leesburg Pike and close to the lower Potomac River Falls. During the Civil War, the church was used by Union troops as a hospital and later as a stable.

Falls Church, Virginia today (left). This Episcopal Church has an active congregation that has worshipped here continuously since 1873. Numerous marked graves are found about the churchyard with the oldest dating back to 1805.

Slave Pen and slave dealers office at 1315 Duke Street, Alexandria, Virginia, circa 1865 (left). This building served as headquarters for the slave trade operations of Isaac Franklin and John Armfield, a partnership formed in 1828. This was one of the largest slave trading companies in the country. The lower buildings on either side of the taller, center building were the actual slave pens. By the time the Civil War started the business was abandoned and during the Federal occupation of Alexandria this building served as a jail for captured Confederate soldiers.

Former slave pen, 1315 Duke Street, Alexandria, Virginia today (right). The slave pen walls on either side were torn down during the Civil War. The building is now a registered National Historic Landmark.

McLean home, Appomattox Court House, Appomattox, Virginia 1865 (right). On April 9th, 1865, this home was used for the surrender of Confederate General Robert E. Lee to General U.S. Grant, representing the Federal government. The actual meeting took place in a room just inside the front door entrance at the top of the stairs.

Print depicting Lee's surrender in the McLean home parlor (left).

The McLean home, Appomattox Court House, Appomattox, Virginia today (left). Around 1892, the home was dismantled and packed for shipping to Chicago for exhibition. The exhibition did not take place and the home remained in the dismantled state for 50 years. In 1940, the property, where the home was originally located, was made into a National Historical Monument under the supervision of the National Park Service. In 1948, the dismantled home was reconstructed on the original site.

Harper House, following the Battle of Bentonville, North Carolina (left). During the waning days of the Civil War, Union General Sherman's march through the south (Carolina Campaign) was met with a determined stand by Confederate General Johnston's forces at Bentonville, North Carolina on March 19, 1865. After three days of battle, with 4,738 causalities on both sides, the Confederate forces withdrew, and later surrendered on April 18, 1865 at the Bennitt Farm by Durham Station, North Carolina (see next). This farm home of John and Amy Harper, built in the late 1850s, played a key role in this battle serving as Union General Slocum's headquarters on the first day of fighting, and later as a field hospital. Over 500 wounded soldiers, including 45 Confederates, were treated at this facility. The Harper family stayed in the area and helped care for the wounded men.

Mock-up of medical treatment area inside the Harper Home, as it might have appeared after the Battle of Bentonville, N.C. (right).

The original Harper Home, Bentonville State Historic Site, Bentonville, North Carolina today (right). This historic site has been designated as a National Historic Landmark and is open to the public with a visitor's center and remnants of the Union earthworks on the surrounding grounds. The location is southeast of Raleigh and south west of Goldsboro, off Highway 701.

The James Bennitt farm home near Durham, South Carolina, circa 1899 (right). In this home, on April 26, 1865, Union General William T. Sherman met with Southern General Joseph E. Johnson. Surrender papers were signed marking the end of the Civil War in the east. This momentous event took place seventeen days after the more famous surrender of Robert E. Lee's Rebel forces at Appomattox Court House, Virginia. (The spelling for Bennitt is the correct English spelling for this family.)

Engraving depicting the surrender event, April 26, 1865 (left).

James Bennitt's home today (left). The photograph was taken from a different perspective. The home itself is a restored reproduction as most of the original home burned down in 1921 (the stone chimney survived). The location is northwest of Durham, North Carolina off Hillsborough Route 70 on 4409 Bennett Memorial Road. The site has been preserved much as it existed during that historic event and a museum is located on the grounds adjacent to the home.

The death bed of President Abraham Lincoln, April, 1865 (left). While Lincoln was watching a play at the Ford's Theater in Washington D.C., John Wilkes Booth crept into Lincoln's unprotected box seat enclosure and shot President Lincoln in the head. Lincoln was not immediately killed so he was taken across the street (10th Street) from the theater to the Peterson Home and laid, diagonally, across a bed in an available room. The mortally wounded Lincoln hung onto to life as his blood stained the pillow that cradled his head. Lincoln soon died and his body was removed. By chance, a photographer (Julius Ulke) was able to set up his camera in the room, soon after Lincoln's body was removed, and record several, historic photographs of the bed. The blood soaked pillow can still be seen on the upper corner of the bed and the hallway through which Lincoln's body was carried can be seen in the right background.

Peterson House today (left). This National Historic Landmark has been faithfully restored, inside and out, to its appearance during the time of the Lincoln assassination. The stairway, and door, seen at the lower right of the photo is the one used by assistants to carry the unconscious Lincoln to a room inside the home."

Reproduction of Lincoln's death bed in the Peterson House, Washington D.C. (above). The pillow under the plastic case was the one Lincoln's head rested on during his last hours of life. The pillow has since been removed to another location.

Modern view of Lincoln's death bed, and room in the Peterson House, Washington D.C. (right). While the bed is a reproduction of the bed seen in the original photograph the room location is the same.

The Old Capitol Prison at First and A Streets, Washington D.C. (right). The building was erected in 1800 and served as a tavern and boarding house. In 1815, after the British burned the U.S. Capitol building, Congress leased this house and used it as a temporary Capitol (it was then known as the Old Capitol). At the start of the Civil War the building was turned into a prison and it was here where military offenders, prisoners of state, and captured rebels were confined. It was also here where the more serious offenders were executed. One of the more infamous Confederate prisoners to be executed was Captain Henry Wirz, former commandant of the Andersonville Prison in Georgia.

Captain Henry Wirtz at the moment of his execution on the grounds of the Old Capitol Prison, November 10, 1865 (left). The soldier on the hanging platform has just released the trap door.

The site of the Old Capitol Prison today (left). First Street in the foreground running from the lower left to right and A Street to the left. Between 1929 and 1932 the current U.S. Supreme Court building was built on the land where the Old Capitol Prison once stood.

The Market Hall at 188 Meeting Street, Charleston, South Carolina as it appeared in 1865 (left). This building, erected in 1841, had three blocks of shopping stalls stretched behind it where the citizens of Charleston were able to obtain fresh meat and produce. Fortunately, this site escaped damage from Union bombardment of Charleston during the Civil War.

Detail of the Market Hall stairway (right).

Market Hall, Charleston, South Carolina today (right). At the time of this photograph, this building served as a museum which contained rare memorabilia of the Civil War as it related to the Southern cause. Note how little has changed in the Market Hall itself and the buildings to the left. The area behind it still has the shopping stalls which serves as a market place for a variety of goods and is well worth a visit while in Charleston.

A semi-submersible boat lies in the mud of the Ashley River, Charleston, South Carolina, circa, 1865. This location was at the end of Tradd Street and the home in the background belonged to John Ashe Alston. The Confederacy had around eight of these ships which could partially submerge and deliver a torpedo at the end of a spar. The ships, called Davids, had limited success by damaging, but not sinking, the Federal gunboat New Ironsides which was part of the Federal fleet blockading Charleston. These Davids were often mistaken for the fully submersible submarines, such as the Hunley, which was able to sink a blockading Union gunboat.

Semi-submersible David location, Charleston, South Carolina today (left). This part of the Ashley River became part of a vast landfill project and the Civil War era water front at this location no longer exists. The John Ashe Alston house, however, still stands at the present day Tradd and Rutledge Streets. Recent evidence indicates that the semi-submersible seen in the original photograph may be buried beneath the street seen in the today photograph.

Mills House hotel, Charleston, South Carolina, circa 1865 (left). During the war, Charleston suffered unrelenting bombardment from Union land based batteries as the damaged buildings surrounding the Mills house show. The heavily bombarded sections were known as the Shell District. The Mills house suffered damage (mainly to the other side which cannot be seen in this photograph) and was closed much of the war.

Modern view of Mills House, Charleston, South Carolina (right). The restored building now has two extra floors and is a Holiday Inn. Because of its central location in Charleston, this hotel is an ideal place to stay while exploring Charleston's rich history.

Confederate earthwork defenses in the White Point Garden (Battery Park) at the foot of East Battery, Charleston, South Carolina, 1865 (right). This location is at the tip of Charleston and the cannons are pointing toward Charleston Bay and Fort Sumter.

Modern view of East Battery park, Charleston, South Carolina (left). This location is at the end of Meeting Street and East Battery Street and has a large park filled with numerous Civil War era cannons and mortars. In addition, this is an excellent location to view Charleston Bay and Fort Sumter. Also, many of the homes in this area have been restored and preserved in their Civil War era state (compare the home at the far right in both photographs).

Looking west on Vendue Range, Charleston South Carolina, circa 1865 (left). Prior to the Civil War, this location was bustling with business activity and pedestrian traffic on the way to the public docks (behind the camera's position). The impressive sidewalk colonnade spoke of better times. Damage from Union bombardment can be seen on the building to the left.

Modern view of Vendue Range, Charleston, South Carolina (right). Directly behind this photographic position is the Water Front Park with excellent views of Charleston Bay. East Bay Street crosses Vendue Range at that point where the white building juts out (upper center) and Vendue Range becomes Queen Street in the distance.

Photo Credits

Sam A. Cooley, US Photographer, Dept. of the South, Unknown location.LC-B171-4018

Brady's photo outfit in front of Petersburg, VA. 1864. LC-B8184 B5077

Fort Riley, Kansas, Alexander Gardner 1867. A rare specimen found on hill above Fort Riely, Kansas/Gardner's Photographic Gallery. LC-USZ62- 11000

Our Photographer at Manassas. Timothy H. O'Sullivan, July 1862. LC-B8184 -651

George Barnard photographing bridge at Strawberry Plains, 20 miles northeast of Knoxville, 1864. LC-2665

Knoxville, Tenn., vicinity. Bridge at Strawberry Plains, 20 miles northeast of Knoxville: camera on tripod at right. George N. Barnard, 1864 LC-8171- 2665

Photographer John Moran, Panama, 1879. LC

John Brown's Fort, 1885. Harpers Ferry Photo Archives

Engine House and Armory at Harpers Ferry, 1862. Harpers Ferry Photo Archives

The Harpers Ferry insurrection engraving. 1859. Harpers Ferry Photo Archives

Abraham Lincoln and supporters in front of Lincoln's home, Springfield, IL Aug. 1860. Chicago Historical Society

Abraham Lincoln's 1st Inauguration. LCUSZ62-22734

President Lincoln's 2nd Inauguration. LC-USZ62-8122

Jefferson Davis being sworn in as President of the Confederacy, Montgomery, AL, Feb. 18, 1861. NA.

Fort Johnson near Charleston, S.C. LC-B8171-3064

Alexandria, Virginia, Marshal House at King and Pitt Street. Created circa 1881-65.LC-8171-2294

Lincoln's White House with Clay Battalion in front. April, 1861. LC

Arlington, Virginia. Guns and gun-crew of Fort Richardson. Created circa 1881-65. 1st Connecticut Artillery drilling at Fort Richardson. LC -2311

Custis-Lee Mansion, or Arlington House, circa 1864. USMHI

Old Stone Church, Centreville, VA. George Barnard, 1862. LC-B8171-0302

Stone Bridge over Bull Run, Manassas Battlefield circa 1862. George Barnard and James Gibson. MCMOLL/ USAMHI

Henry Home, Manassas Battlefield, March 1862. LC-B8171-320

Bull Run, Virginia. Matthews or Stone House, photographed in July, 1861.LC-0318

Bull Run Monument Dedication, June, 1865. Photographer William Morris Smith.LC-B8171-7362

Pittsburg Landing along the Tennessee River, April, April 1862. MCMOLL/USAMHI

Frederick, Maryland, Union troops on Market Street, February 22, 1862. From the Benjamin Rosenstock collection Catalog No.P0244. Courtesy of the Historical Society of Frederick County, Maryland.

Chatham or Lacy House, Fredericksburg, VA, circa 1862. LC- 697

Frederick, Maryland, Confederate troops marching west on Patrick Street, Sep. 12, 1862. From the Benjamin Rosenstock collection, Catalog No. P0241. Courtesy of the Historical Society of Frederick County, Maryland

Confederate dead on the Antietam battlefield with Dunker Church in background, Sep. 19, 1862. Gardner stereo. #562, MCMOLL/USAMHI

Dead Confederate soldiers after the battle of Antietam.Alexander Gardner, September, 1863. LC-B8171-560

Burnside Bridge, view looking westward. Sep. 21, 1862 Gibson, stereo LC-614

View of Antietam battlefield, Sep. 17, 1862. LC-B8171- 671

Knap's Battery on the Antietam Battlefield, Gardner stereo. Sep. 19, 1862. LC-577

Confederate dead in Bloody Lane, Antietam battlefield. MCMOLL/USAMHI

Scene of Sedgwick's advance and the grave of Lt. John A. Clark, 7th Mich. View looking toward West Woods and Miller's fields, Sep. 19, 1862. Gardner stereo. LC-551

Union burial party. Antietam.Gardner stereo LC-561

Village of Sharpsburg looking down Hall St. Sep. 21, 1862. LC-599

President Lincoln, General McClellan and others at Fifth Corps headquarters. Gardner, Oct. 3, 1862. LC-7951

Fairfax, Virginia, Fairfax Court House, The courthouse photographed by Timothy H. O'Sullivan June, 1863. LC- 0298

Union breastworks on Little Round Top. Gardner stereo, July 6, 1863. LC-247

Confederate dead at the base of Little Round Top after the Battle of Gettysburg. Alexander Gardner, July 6, 1863. Stereo LC--65

Confederate dead gathered for burial at edge of Rose Woods. Gardner stereo, July 5, 1863. LC-268

Confederate dead gathered for burial at edge of Rose Woods. Gardner stereo, July 5, 1863. LC-235

Confederate soldiers captured at Gettysburg on Seminary Ridge. Brady stereo, July 15, 1863. LC-2397

Meade's headquarters, Gettysburg, Penn., Alexander Gardner, stereo July 6, 1863. LC-259

The Lutheran Seminary, view from east. July 15, 1863. Brady stereo. LC-2393

The Thompson house, Lee's headquarters, Gettysburg, July 15, 1863. Brady stereo, LC-407

Breastworks on Culp's Hill occupied by 102nd NY Reg. July, 15, 1863. Brady stereo. NA111-SC-114770

View looking north on Baltimore St. LC-B818-10001

Dedication ceremonies at Soldiers National Cemetery. Nov. 19, 1863. LC-1160

Murfreesboro Courthouse. MCMOLL/USAMHI

Wounded soldiers from the Battle's of the Wilderness and Spotsylvania, 1864. Brady.LC- -2507

Wounded soldiers from the Battle's of the Wilderness and Spotsylvania, 1864. Brady.LC-B8184 8462

Wall at Marye's Heights, Fredericksburg, VA with Rebel dead following the Battle of Chancellorsville. MCMOLL/USAMHI

Camp of 44th NY overlooking Alexandria, VA. Brady panoramic series. NA111-B-193 or 145

Two views of Andersonville Prison, a Confederate prison for Union prisoner. Circa 1863. USAMHI

Fort Desperate, Port Hudson, Louisiana. MCMOLL/USAMHI

General Grant on Lookout Mountain following battle of Chattanooga.LC-US262

Pulpit Rock on Lookout Mountain with signal station. LC-3661

General Hooker on Lookout Rock. USAMHI

General McCallum and aide on Lookout Mountain. LC-USZ62

Cavalryman on Lookout Mountain. USAMHI

Behind Union Lines with Shirley House, Vicksburg, Mississippi. Vicksuburg County Courthouse and Museum.

U.S.S. Cairo ironclad gunboat on Mississippi River. LC-8184-3135

Alfred Waud drawing of Spotsylvania Battlefield, May 12, 1864. LC-USZ62-7047

Massaponax Church, May 21, 1865. LC-729

General Grant and staff at Massaponax Church, May 21, 1865. LC-732

Mortar position on the Petersburg Siege Lines, September, 1864. Alexander Gardner. LC-7394

The Crater, Petersburg Battlefield, circa 1865. USAMHI

Cowan's Union Battery in captured Confederate Battery on eastern front, Petersburg, VA.June 20, 1864, Brady. MCMOLL/USAMHI

Brady with Union battery in captured Confederate battery, Petersburg. MCMOLL/USAMHI

Captured Confederate fort on outskirts of Atlanta, GA, 1865. LC -B635

Interior of Fort McAllister, Dec. 1864. LC-4010

Savannah, Ga., vicinity. Confederate gun at Fort McAllister, December, 1865. LC-4002

Fort Pulaski interior view. LC-B8171-194

Sally Port to Fort Delaware, circa 1865. Delaware Historical Society

Battery Buchanan at Fort Fisher, NC. Courtesy of the N.C. Office of Archives and History N.69.7.422

Interior views of Fort Fisher. LC-B8171-7056 and LCB8171-7057

Falls Church, circa 1863. MCMOLL/ USMHI

Alexandria, Virginia, Price, Birch & Co., dealers in slaves at 283 Duke St. Photographed by William Pywell 1863. LC -1003

McLean Home site of Lee's surrender, Appomattox Court House, VA. LC-7292

Harper Home, Bentonville, NC following the battle of Bentonville, April, 1865. Western Reserve Historical Society

James Bennitt farm home, Durham Station, NC. LC-ZGZ-108506

President Lincoln's deathbed in Peterson House, Washington D.C. Meserve-Kunhardt Collection.

Old Capitol Prison. LC-1019

Old Capitol Prison execution of Henry Wirz. LC-7754

Charleston, South Carolina. The old Market House at 188 Meeting Street. Created in 1865.

Semi-submersible in mud of Ashley River at foot of Tradd St. NA

Mill Hotel, Charleston, S.C. LC-3078

Confederate earthwork defenses at White Point Garden (Battery Park) Charleston, S.C. NA

Looking west on Vendue Range, Charleston , S.C. NA

Bibliography

Civil War era photographs appear in almost every book written on the subject. Some of these images are of excellent quality and some are not. The information about the photos can be either accurate or inaccurate. I have limited my bibliography to those books that, in my estimation, have the most accurate information and/or reproduce the best quality photographs.

The one source that I recommend for the largest collection of Civil War era images is:

Davis, William C. and Wiley, Bell L., *Civil War Album, Complete Photographic History of the Civil War*, Tess Press. 1981 – 1984

This book is a big, heavy, and expensive compilation of six previous, separate, volumes that encompasses the entire Civil War. It was produced under the direction of the National Historic Society. The contents are an excellent resource for historical information and photographs.

An excellent, smaller, and less expensive resource is:

Time Life Books Editors, *An Illustrated History of the Civil War, Images of an American Tragedy,* 2000

A recent book on Matthew Brady's work contains a wealth of accurate information on a variety of Brady's photographs. This is a good choice for those who want to know more about this famous photographer.

Garrison, Webb, *Brady's Civil War, A collection of memorable Civil War images photographed by Matthew Brady and his assistants.*

A Salamander Book published by The Lyons Press, 2000,

A complete book of Then and Now Civil War photographs of Charleston, South Carolina is:

Thomas, Jack, *Charleston at War, The Photographic Record 1860-1865*, Thomas Publications, 2000.

Besides Brady, there are other photographers (former Brady assistants) whose collective body of work is an invaluable resource. The following books present excellent reproductions of their work and can be purchased in paperback versions:

Gardner, Alexander, *Gardner's Photographic Sketch Book of the Civil War*, Dover Publications, 1959

Russell, Andrew J., *Russell's Civil War Photographs,* Dover Publications, 1982

Barnard, George N., *Photographic Views of Sherman's Campaign*, Dover Publications 1977

Since the majority of Civil War photographs were made with the stereographic camera the following two-volume set is an excellent addition to this subject. What is so good about these books is the wealth of newly presented information and accompanying stereo glasses, which allows the reader to see the images in three dimensions. When looking at these images one can almost imagine being there at the time the photo was made:

Zeller, Bob, *The Civil War in Depth, History in 3-D,* Volume I and II, Chronicle Books, 1997 & 2000

Since Abraham Lincoln was the focal point of the Civil War many books, with photographs, have been written about him. The following is, in my estimation, one of the best productions:

Kunhardt Jr., Philip B., Kunhardt, Philip B. III, and Kunhardt, Peter W., *Lincoln, An Illustrated Biography*, Alfred A. Knopf, Inc, 1992

If one wants to learn more about Civil War photography the following source is a good starting point:

Kelbaugh, Ross J., *Introduction to Civil War Photography,* Thomas Publications, 1991.

The best source for detailed information and photographs concerning the forts built around Washington D.C. during the Civil War is:

Cooling III, Benjamin Franklin and Owen II, Walton H., *Mr. Lincoln's Forts, A Guide to the Civil War Defenses of Washington,*

White Maine Publishing Company, Inc., 1988

For those who are interested in American combat photography with more detailed information about those photographers of the Civil War try:

Moyes, Norman B. *American Combat Photography, From the Civil War to the Gulf War,* Metro Books, 2001

Last, but not least, the books that set the record straight for so many Civil War photographs. Historian William A. Frassanito's four volumes which present detailed evidence for the locations of Civil War photographs. These books sparked my interest, and desire, to know more on the subject. I highly recommend these books for accurate information and directions to the photographic locations:

Frassanito, William A., Antietam, *The Photographic Legacy of America's Bloodiest Day,* Charles Scribner's Sons, 1978

Frassanito, William A., Antietam, Gettysburg, *A Journey in Time,* Charles Scribner's Sons, 1975

Frassanito, William A., Antietam, *Grant and Lee, The Virginia Campaigns 1864-1865,* Charles Scribner's Sons, 1983

Frassanito, William A., *Early Photography at Gettysburg,* Thomas Publications, 1995

Listings of Civil War sites on the web can be found in:

Carter, Alice E. and Thomas, William G., *The Civil War on the Web, A Guide to the Very Best Sites,* Scholarly Resources Inc., 2001

Today, the art of collodion or Wet- Plate Collodion photography is maintained by a few, dedicated, and talented artisans. Their web sites are a valuable source of information about view cameras and the process of producing photographs using the same techniques used by Civil War photographers:

www.collodion-artist.com/ Web site for Will Dunniway, Wet-Plate Collodion artist

www.companyphotographer.com/ Web site for Wayne L. Pierce, Wet-Plate Collodion artist

www.cwreenactors.com/collodion/index.php/ Web site for R.Z. Szabo, Wet-Plate Collodion artist

Index